AF353226

MOVE
MOUNTAINS
ONE STORY AT A TIME

MOVE MOUNTAINS

ONE STORY AT A TIME

By

Mukesh Kulothia
Deepak Sharma

Gullybaba Publishing House Pvt. Ltd.
ISO 9001 & ISO 14001 CERTIFIED CO.

PUBLICATION

Published under the faithful principles of

Gullybaba Publishing House Pvt. Ltd.

Regd. Office: 2525/193, 1st Floor, Onkar Nagar-A,
Tri Nagar, Delhi-110035,
Ph.: 09350849407, 09312235086
Branch Office: 1A/2A, 20, Hari Sadan, Ansari Road,
Daryaganj, New Delhi-110002, **Ph.:** 011-23239034, 011-45794768

First Edition: 2019

ISBN: 978-93-88149-61-7

All Rights Reserved

All the ideas and thoughts in this book are given by the authors and they are responsible for the treatise, facts and dialogues used in this book. They are also responsible for the used pictures and the permission to use them in this book. All rights of this book are reserved with the authors. The publisher does not have any responsibility for the above-mentioned matters. No part of this publication may be reproduced, distributed, or transmitted in any form or by any means, including photocopying, recording or other electronic method without the prior written permission of the publisher and the authors.

Layout Design: Gullybaba Publishing House Pvt. Ltd.

Print: Repro Knowledgecast Ltd.

Contents

Foreword

What a delight it is to read a bunch of stories that bring out significant lessons of life in a simple, yet highly effective way. It is difficult not to see the fifty two short stories as a pack of cards that unfolds a lovely lesson with every card. Shuffle them any which way and you will be dealt with a valuable life lesson.

The book encourages you to work on yourself and realize your potential through a set of stories and the lessons thereupon. My personal favorite is to be a leader, see the invisible. At the ground breaking ceremony of the Walt Disney world, when a reporter asks Walt Disney's nephew how tragic it was that Walt wasn't alive to see his dream come to life, the nephew replied: Oh, but you are wrong. He saw it that is why you are seeing it. The underlying message is at once simple and profound. Visionaries have the ability to see things the way they would eventually unfold and then they set themselves the task to make it happen. Put together, purpose and passion can change the world, and if done with compassion, the world is necessarily changed for the better.

Misinterpreting the oft quoted axiom, Knowledge is power; people often tend to zealously guard their knowledge, information, refusing to share it with others. Remember, knowledge is communicable, wisdom is not. The honey bee reminds us in the sixth story, Skill Plus Yourself, that a man can only steal my honey, not the art of making honey! Others can use your notes, examples, presentations, but they cannot explain what YOU have lived and experienced. Share your knowledge and experience with others and you will, in turn, learn from them. Everyone and everything around us has something to teach us, provided we have an open heart and an open mind. Love begets love and trust begets trust. The key, therefore, is to stop being afraid of looking or being vulnerable and love and trust others around us. Yes, we may get hurt in the process every once in a while, but that too makes us stronger as a person.

Talking of hurt, the thirty first story reminds us that no one can hurt you without your consent. The thirty fifth story reaffirms the lesson when Buddha refuses to be rattled by the harsh words thrown at him. Gandhi reminded us that no one can take our self-respect away if we don't give it to them! In my own experiences I have realised that what others think of you is none of your business. Let them stay with their thoughts, while you keep yours. This is not to say that you should not be open to constructive feedbacks but to remind you that don't let those remarks let you think less of yourself. Your quest in life should be to know yourself and seek self-improvement perpetually, and not to wonder over what others are thinking or saying about you.

All in all, the book opens up a world of myriad possibilities and life lessons, interwoven into delightful stories. From the *Panchatantra* to the *Jataka* tales to the Arabian Nights, storytelling has had a profound impact on us. So grab a copy of this book, open any page and start reading; and I assure you that it will make you think.

– Prof. Himanshu Rai

Preface

To both of us, life gave ample opportunities to experiment and see the impact of stories on the growth of individuals, families and organizations. Our one year stint together in the top three officers at Toastmasters International's District 41 was a cherry on the cake. Here, we successfully experimented on the power of motivation especially through stories - fables, anecdotes, sharing of real life experiences, incidents or fictions! We far exceeded the global growth numbers in number of membership payments, clubs as well as the Distinguished Clubs. District 41 became #1 in the world by breaking all the records in all the three criteria.

Our habit of reading and sharing stories to all made a significant impact in our personal and professional lives. The stories ignite motivation in people and are tools of sustainable growth to individuals and teams. Thus this book 'MOVE MOUNTAINS – ONE STORY AT A TIME' – a collection of stories that touch hearts and help people reach their dreams.

Stories can inspire, ignite and impact human beings to an extent that we cannot even imagine. . Well told stories ensure clarity like no other tool of communication and wider acceptance of viewpoints. The formula, "Tell a story and make a point" ensures flawless communication and adoption of your vision by the people

People have dreams and occasionally, especially in the beginning they get excited about their dreams. But soon when people don't see any movement in the direction of fulfilling their dreams and they get frustrated. People start feeling as if the dreams are big mountains which they can't move. Result - people give up and dreams wither. Initially they give up on the dreams and then gradually they also give up the habit of dreaming. This is sad; really sad and unfortunate.

This book is a humble attempt to help you not only to see big dreams but stay charged up, take actions and move your mountain like dreams and goals to the done state. In case your goals are not individual but organizational, you can motivate your teams to take actions, embrace excellence and go for the glory.

We congratulate you on your decision to pick this book up and sincerely hope that it makes a difference to your life and to the lives of other people around. 52 stories in the book signify 52 weeks i.e. a year full of motivation, happiness and success.

This book is an ideal gift to your friends and colleagues on New Year or on their birthdays - let your good wishes for them become tangible. Let they carry your good wishes in their hand, head and heart in shape of this book. If you are an entrepreneur or a manager in a company - how about all your people getting a copy of it!

Oh, did we tell you that this book gives you full flexibility to pick up any story any day, read and imagine the connection in your life or work. We encourage you to share the stories with your friends, family and colleagues but keep the book in your collection so that you have the access to the motivation mantras.

Wishing you a life full of success and happiness!

– Mukesh & Deepak

Gratitude

Today when we write this page, we feel indebted to so many wonderful story tellers from our childhood to today at home, schools and organizations we served at. Many people have told us and taught us the power of stories in theory and practice. Heartfelt thanks to those unsung inspiring story tellers.

People, who touched our lives in Toastmasters International, deserve special thanks. Toastmasters across the world have motivated us in more ways than we can write.

Our free, fantastic and first editor Shakthi Priya Gowri is a genius. Many thanks to her for the wonderful assistance throughout the journey.

Some other awesome helping hearts who we must thank are Dr Aparna Makkar, Mrs Vandana Joshi and Ms Honey Khanduja. They are the best content curators.

Prof Himanshu Rai is a role model to many thousands of people. I (Mukesh) got an opportunity to have him as my teacher at Indian Institute of Management, Lucknow and getting him to write the Foreward of this book is a dream come true in itself. Prof Rai, didn't just write the Foreward but gave very valuable feedback on many aspects to make this book a masterpiece. Gratitude!

There are no words for our publisher **Gullybaba Publishing House Pvt Ltd,** especially **Mr. Dinesh Verma** for supporting and guiding us in hassle free book publishing.

Deep gratitude to our families for encouraging and contributing in many ways to make this book a reality.

We are sure this book will impact and bring positive change in your life.

Thank you for picking up your copy. Enjoy reading – we would love to connect with you whenever and wherever life presents an opportunity for the same.

1

The Old Man And The Violin!

Many years ago a rich industrialist was on his deathbed. As his last wish, he requested his wife to auction all his materialistic collections and donate the money received to a children charity. She called an auctioneer to do the needful. As the auction came to close, the tired auctioneer held up a battered, dusty violin and asked mockingly, "what am I bid for this? Let's start with ₹500. No takers; Okay ₹300; Still no takers; How about ₹100?" The auctioneer laughed and turned to put the violin aside.

A faint cracked voice interrupted the laughter, "Excuse me, may I have a moment of your time?" A bent old man shuffled up to the auctioneer and reached for the violin with a thin pale hand. With his back to the audience, the old man first cleaned the dust from the violin with his handkerchief, plucked each string and expertly adjusted the tuning pegs. Then he placed the violin under his chin and began to play.

Lovely music filled the room; people were mesmerized and sat frozen with awe as the old man played it with a heavenly solo. After playing it beautifully, he handed it over to the auctioneer and walked out of the door slowly as everyone burst into a spontaneous applause.

The auctioneer held up the old violin again and shouted, "Now what am I bid for this violin?" Somebody said ₹1000, a voice came ₹1500; another said ₹2000 and so on. Finally it was sold for ₹10000.

This story paints a vivid picture of the concept of value and how to maximize it. The value of the same violin increased from almost zero to ₹10000 just by a little fine tuning and adjustment. Isn't it the same with us? We keep on moving from day to day without shedding the dust of conditioning and tuning our skills. We live the same day in the same way for months and years. Then, we wonder why we are not getting the desired results. Like this violin, everyone has lot of hidden potential. It is our personal responsibility to understand and realize the potential. Just the way we upgrade our devices, our mind and body also need consistent upgrading. If we don't feed and nurture our mind how will it support us in achieving our goals?

Today is the day we can start dusting off the beliefs which might have held us back in the past. With seemingly small but regular actions we can start tuning the pegs of life to create some musical and magical results.

When you improve a little each day, eventually big things occur.

– John Wooden

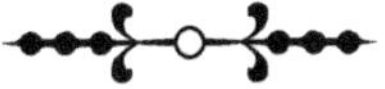

2

Man With A Dream
Will Not Be Denied!

As a horse trainer, young Monty's father was moving from stable to stable, ranch to ranch, training horses. Thus, the boy's school career was often interrupted due to the family's movement from town to town. One day, his school teacher asked the students to write about what they wanted to be when they grew up. Monty did not hesitate even a minute and wrote a seven-page long paper about his dream to be the owner of a horse ranch. He was very meticulous about many details and drew locations of buildings, stables and even a detailed house plan. Two days later, the teacher returned his paper with the letter "F" on the front page. After the class, he asked the teacher: "Why did I get an F?" The teacher responded: "This dream is so unrealistic for a boy like you, who has no money, no resources and comes from a wandering family. There is no possibility that you will reach your great dream any day." The teacher offered him to rewrite the paper with a more realistic attitude.

The boy went home and sought his father's advice on how he should act in response to this. The father answered: "This decision is very important for you and you have to make your own mind on this." After few days the boy brought the same paper to his teacher. Not a single change was made. He said: "Teacher, respectfully, you can keep your F and I will keep my dream."

Many years later, that teacher was invited by Monty Roberts to his 4,000-square-feet house in the middle of 200-acre horse ranch and he still had that school paper with an F, which now is framed over the fireplace.

Walt Disney's words, "If you can dream it, you can achieve it" have immense power. Dreaming was always out of school and college syllabus; let this be a part of our life syllabus. As per the social conditioning, most of us believe that life is all about formal education, 9 to 6 job, getting married, having kids and then making them do the whole cycle again.

Life is actually about dreaming and creating things for the world. Only human beings have the power to dream and with this power we can empower ourselves to achieve anything in our life.

Man With A Dream Will Not Be Denied!

Monty Robert was able to achieve his dream because he was able to see and protect his dream. Let us dream BIG, protect it and achieve the same!

If people are not laughing on your dreams, your dreams are too small.

– Azim Premji

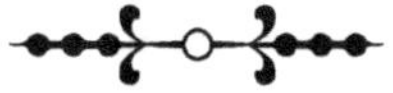

3

Don't Be A Dog, Chasing Vehicles!

Once, a farmer had a dog who used to sit by the roadside waiting for vehicles to come around. Every single time a vehicle came, the dog, without fail, would run down the road, barking and trying to overtake it.

One day a neighbor asked the farmer, "Do you think your dog is ever going to catch a vehicle?"

The farmer smiled and replied, "That is not what bothers me. What concerns me is - what would it do if it ever catches one!"

Most of us love to have goals and we toil for something or the other. But do we really know what it is we are running for? Is it worth the run? Many people in life end up pursuing meaningless goals just like that dog. So how do we assure that we are fighting for something purposeful? God has given us a gift of being human and the difference between human and animal is that we have capability of setting worthy goals and achieving those. Having a dream gives us wings to fly but what actually makes us fly is having a clear goal and plan to finish many seemingly insignificant tasks which when done consistently, produce humongous results.

Every Sunday night, let us give a gift of 30 minutes to ourselves. Sit in a quiet place and think on the worthwhile goals we want to reach this week, month or year.

Voila - Magic! Our actions will have a velocity towards our dreams and we will see a compounding effect of the small wins everyday towards our BIG dreams. If we are consistent in making the time of 30 minutes for ourselves every week - the progress will certainly amaze us.

Abraham Lincoln said, **"A goal properly set is halfway done."** *Let us invest time in setting and reviewing our goals on regular basis. We can break big tasks into smaller chunks and go on to tick them off the list one by one.*

But, some of the most significant questions which we must ask ourselves often in life are "Is this goal worth chasing? What contributions will it make to me and the society once reached"?

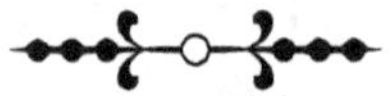

4

To Be A Leader:
See The Invisible!

Mr. Walt Disney went from person to person with his idea of Mickey-Mouse and everyone rejected the idea, but he kept on going till somebody finally said that it was a great idea. Here is a man who turned a cartoon mouse into an international multi-billion dollar enterprise. Walt's vision of creating a fantasy playground for children of all age groups was very vivid; he converted thousands of acres of California farmland into the world's first successful theme park- Disneyland. Walt Disney World in Orlando, wasn't near completion until long after Mr. Disney passed away. At the groundbreaking ceremony for Walt Disney World, a reporter addressed Roy Disney, Walt's nephew stating that it was too sad that Walt wasn't alive to see his dream come to life.

Roy smiled at the reporter and said, "Oh but you are wrong. He saw it that is why you are seeing it."

To achieve any dream or goal you have to see it much before it happens. Everything in the world happens twice, once within your mind and then in reality.

If we want things to happen in our lives, it is very important for us to have a vision and vision is "seeing the invisible". Disney World was part of Walt Disney's grand vision. He saw all these happening long before any of us did. Many a times you can see things for yourself, but due to lack of clarity and plan, we give up on the way. People will curse you for talking impossible. But if you can see the vision, hold on. Break the huge vision into smaller pieces of doable tasks. Make a list and get started on those. All of us have some or the other experience in our lives where we wanted to achieve something badly, all our senses were active to see, smell, touch and feel the unhappened with vividness; the things happened.

Let us invest time, energy and money in our ability to see the invisible, the yet to happen things. Invest in our leadership capability development and we can not only succeed in our lives but can also offer greater service to the world around because the world needs leaders today, more than ever before.

People who have the ability to see a vision are the ones who make great things happen and are called visionary leaders. We can develop this art with conscious efforts and be a leader, people would love to follow.

Vision is the art of seeing things invisible to others.

— *Jonathan Swift*

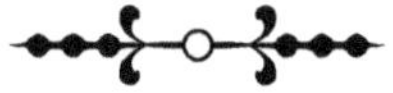

5

Answer Is In Your Hands!

In a small village, lived a saint who was worshipped by all. People used to go to him with their problems and he always had a solution for them. Everyone believed that the saint could look into the future and predict it for them. In the same village, there lived a boy who was very jealous of the saint's popularity. To prove the saint wrong, he challenged the worshipped. He claimed that in front of the whole village, he would prove 'the saint was an imposter and knew nothing about the future'.

The boy appeared in front of the saint and his devotees, hiding a little bird in his fist. He asked the saint to guess what was he holding?

The saint said "It's indeed a pleasant sight to see a bird in human's hand."

The boy was surprised that the saint could guess it right.

In front of the whole village, the boy's reputation was at stake so he asked yet another question to the saint "can you tell if the bird is dead or alive?"

The boy's plan was to let it fly off if the saint said its dead and to kill the bird by squeezing the fist if the saint said it was alive. This way he could prove that the saint was lying.

To this, the saint said, "The answer is in your hand my son. If you wish, you can let the bird live and if you want, you can kill it."

Friends, most often the answers to our dreams and goals are in our hands. Our success and failure in any venture is a function of our choices.

Today you chose to read this book and sure, in some way or the other, this will create some difference in your life. Instead of finding answers outside and blaming external environment for our failures, remember we can make the bird of our dreams fly or we can kill the same by our own decision. Maybe some of the choices are made unknowingly but know that there are U turns on the roads of life. Nobody in the world should be blamed for anything that happens in our lives. There will always be naysayers, however, it is totally up to us whether we listen to them or not.

Our success can only be chiseled by our choices and actions. Let us choose wisely and act quickly.

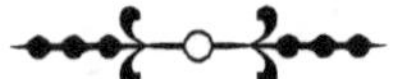

6

Skill Plus Yourself!

Once a bird asked a bee, "You prepare the honey after continuous hard work. But men steal that in a jiffy. Don't you feel sad?"

The bee replied, "Never. A man can only steal my honey, not the art of making honey."

What a wonderful lesson! We must invest money, time and energy in self-development and learn to make honey in life. The honey which makes us healthy, wealthy and happy; the honey which gives us confidence to become a linchpin in organizations we work and in the families we live.

If we were to put this in three beautiful words, 'Skill Plus Yourself'. This is not only good to do but given the times we live in, it is a must-do thing. Today, it's really difficult to do business with yesterday's tools and ways. Let us, identify the skill we want to grow in and get started! Martin Luther once said,

"If you can't fly, then run

If you can't run, then walk

If you can't walk, then crawl

But whatever you do keep moving forward."

In today's times we can keep moving forward only when we keep refining our skills, attitude and behavior. Of course, one step at a time is the way to make it happen but even before the step, let us identify one skill which can make maximum impact in our career or life and make the decision to ace this. Many a times, we are just one skill away from success of our dreams.

Let the identification and pursuit of that one skill be our priority.

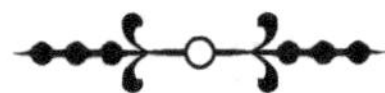

7

Make A Difference
Small Or Big!

There was a boy, out on his morning walk at a beautiful beach. He was enjoying the beauty of the rising sun and the cool breeze flowing against his face. He saw that along with the morning tide, came hundreds of starfish. When the tide receded, they were left behind and with the morning sun rays, they would die. The tide was fresh and the starfish were alive. The boy took a few steps, picked one and threw it into the water. He did that repeatedly. Right behind him there was another person who couldn't understand what this boy was doing. He caught up with him and asked, "What are you doing? There are hundreds of starfish. How many can you help? What difference does it make?" The boy, walked two steps, picked up another one, threw it into the water, and said, "It makes a difference to this one."

Wow! What a thought! we believe, at some or the other time we have been at the place of the starfish. Someone came in our life and made a difference with the much needed help and guidance. You can ask a question to yourself and come up with few names of those starfish saver kind of people but even more important question is - who are you helping to? What difference are you making in the lives of the people around? At times, we ourselves dwarf our own good work by assuming the acts of goodness as tiny.

Henceforth, let us remember this story; do whatever we can to whoever we can and wherever we can without really worrying for the scale. The size of the difference is not that important at the start, what matters is the consistency with which we are striking the hammer of difference. Let's resolve to make these seemingly small differences in the lives of people around without being judgmental on the size of the impact.

If everyone made a small difference, we would end up making a big difference in the world, wouldn't we?

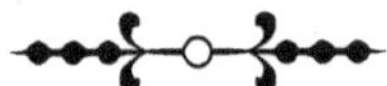

8

Even If You See The Glass As Half Full - It's Still Theory!

A father came home after a long tiring day at his office. He poured a glass of water to himself, sat on a chair and started sipping while browsing through his phone. He was done with almost half of it and there came his three year old prep-school going daughter, straight in the lap of her daddy. Father asked a really heavy leadership question - "baby, is the glass half full or half empty?"

The girl jumped out of the daddy's lap, rushed to other room in the house, got her water bottle from the little school bag. Opened it, poured water in the glass and said, "It's neither half full nor half empty - this is completely full, daddy"!

What a perspective! I see, most of us get happy with the response of glass being half full; and we boast about being a positive thinker. Yet, we must realize that half empty or half full, whatever is the response- it's still theory. Need of the hour is - Action. Action is the foundational key to success. Action oriented people make things happen and succeed like genius. Let's get into the habit of acting really fast. As soon as we get an idea to make a difference in our life or the world around – let us just jump out of the seat and do it.

Let us go beyond theory and do the due. Let us stop talking and start doing. If we fail, we will gain experience; if we win, we will make a difference. Action is really the king.

Remember, what the world hero of basketball said,

I have missed more than 9000 shots in my career. I have lost almost 300 games. 26 times, I have been trusted to take the game winning shot and missed. I have failed over and over in my life. And that is why I succeed.

– Michael Jordan

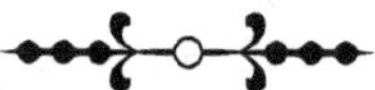

9

What Goes Around, Comes Around!

A farmer used to sell one pound of butter to a baker every day. One day, the baker decided to weigh the butter to see if he was getting a pound and ended up finding that the butter weighed less than a pound. This made the baker furious and he took the farmer to court.

During the hearing, the judge asked the farmer if he was using any measure. The farmer replied, "Sir, I am an illiterate person. I don't have a proper measure, but I do have a scale." The judge asked, "Then how do you know that your scale is correct?" The farmer replied "Your Honor, long before the baker started buying butter from me, I have been buying a pound of bread loaf from him. Every day when the baker brings the bread, I put it on the scale and give him the same weight of butter. If anyone is to be blamed for unfair weight, it is the baker."

We get back in life what we give to others. Whenever we take an action, let us ask ourselves the question: "Are we giving fair value for the wages or the money we hope to make?" Even if we are doing any voluntary task, let us always try to give more and that is the process of getting back more. Giving is indeed receiving. To start with, we can start giving more smiles and kindness - we will see the magic happening.

Remember what lord Krishna said in Gita, ***"If you start giving more than you get, soon you will start getting more than you give".***

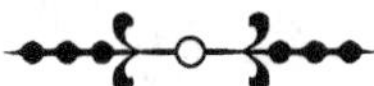

10

Don't Leave A Scar!

There was a little boy, who had a bad temper. Once, his father decided to mend his son's behavior. He gave a bag full of nails to his son and told him that every time he lost his temper, he must hammer a nail into the fence.

On the first day, the boy had driven 17 nails into the fence. Over the next few weeks, as he learned to control his anger, the number of nails hammered gradually dwindled down. He discovered that it was easier to hold his temper than to drive those nails into the fence.

Finally came a day, when the boy didn't lose his temper at all. He told his father about it and the father suggested that the boy should now pull out one nail for each day that he was able to hold his temper.

The days passed and the young boy was finally able to tell his father that all the nails were gone. The father took his son by the hand and led him to the fence. He said "You have done well, my son, but look at the holes in the fence. The fence will never be the same. When you say things in anger, they leave scars just like these."

We meet many people, who have this challenge of losing their temperament, which results into losing relationships. The world is moving towards instant gratifications. We download some apps and can do many things. However, the only thing that can never be done by apps, is building long-term relationships. Relationships are nurtured by healing people from their problems and sorrows. The world loves to do business with nice people. This can only happen when we work on our temperament. Many a times in our pressure cooker situations, we lose temper and say words that leave life-long scar on other people. Isn't it a good idea to keep calm and think before speaking? Our words have power to change the world, let us use them carefully.

In a gentle way, you can shake the world.

– Mahatma Gandhi

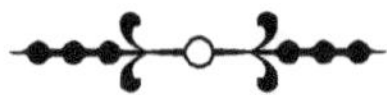

11

Never Give Up!

On a cold wintery night, two frogs, a big fat one and a tiny little one, were enjoying in the kitchen of a house. Both the frogs could smell fragrance of milk in a pail nearby and incidentally, the pail was not covered. Both the brothers were peeping into the pail and fell into the milk pail one after the other.

The pail had slippery sides. They swam and swam for hours to get out. Exhausted, the big frog moaned, *'Little brother frog, I am giving up'* and it sank to the bottom of the pail. The little frog thought, *'If I give up I will die for sure, so I must keep on swimming'*.

Two hours passed and the little frog thought it could do no more. But as it thought of its dead brother frog, it roused its will saying, *'To give up is certain death. I will keep on paddling until I die. I will not give up trying, for while there is life there is still hope'.*

Fueled with determination, the little frog kept on paddling. After hours, when it felt paralyzed with fatigue and could paddle no more, it suddenly felt a big lump under its feet. His incessant paddling had churned the milk into butter. Standing on the butter mound with great joy, the little frog leaped from the milk pail to freedom.

We all are in slippery milk pails of life, trying to get free from obstacles and succeed in the battle like the two frogs. Most people give up trying and fail like the big frog. But we must learn to persevere in our efforts towards our goals, as the little frog did. The people who latch on to their dreams and don't give up move mountains. People, who have faced bigger obstacles and didn't give up, have achieved bigger results. Remember, it's the darkest before the dawn. Whenever we find ourselves in problems, let us start kicking and keep kicking until we are out in the sunshine.

A winner is a dreamer who never gives up.

— **Nelson Mandela**

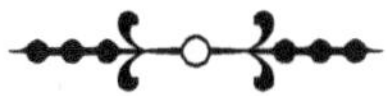

12

When To Look At The Mirror And When At The Window!

D r Abdul Kalam was one of the finest Presidents India ever had. He fondly shared a story from his life as a scientist which teaches an awesome leadership lesson.

In the early days of his career as a scientist, he was working as a Project Manager for a Satellite Launch Vehicle (SLV) program and was leading a team to put a satellite in an orbit. On the day of the launch, all went well for a while, but eventually the satellite plunged into the earth. The launch had failed. His boss Dr Satish Dhawan, calmly stepped into the sea of cameras and microphones and accepted full responsibility of the failure. He assured people that he with his team will work harder and make it a success soon. Within a year, the team tried again and succeeded in meeting the objective of putting satellite in the orbit. This time, Dr Dhawan asked Dr Kalam to go to the media and conduct the press conference. Dr Dhawan gave all the accolades to Dr Kalam and made him a hero. Dr Kalam shared this story fondly with media and students across the world, with a simple takeaway: 'Leaders share the credit of success and accept the responsibility of failure'.

Next time when we succeed, we need to find people we should give credit to; whereas in case of a failure, let us stand firm and accept the full responsibility. Momentarily, accepting the responsibility of a team failure may hurt our ego a bit, but it helps us gain people by our side who become dedicated to the cause. These people will not only make us succeed in bigger ventures of our work and life, but may also become fans of our leadership style.

When our team fails, let us look at the mirror; when our team succeeds, let us look at the window.

13

Embrace The Challenges And Don't Be Too Kind!

A man found a cocoon of a butterfly. One day a small opening appeared.

He sat and watched the butterfly for several hours as it struggled to squeeze its body through the tiny hole.

Then it stopped, as if it couldn't go further.

The man then decided to help the butterfly. He took a pair of scissors and snipped off the remaining bits of cocoon.

The butterfly emerged easily, but it had a swollen body and shriveled wings.

The man continued to watch it, expecting that any minute the wings would enlarge and expand enough to support the body.

Neither happened!

In fact the butterfly spent the rest of its life crawling around. It lost its ability to fly and subsequently gave up the life.

The man in his kindness and haste did not understand that the restricting cocoon and the struggle required by the butterfly to get through the opening was a way of forcing the fluid from the body into the wings so that it would be ready for flight once that was achieved.

Sometimes struggles are exactly what we need in our lives. Going through life with no obstacles would cripple us. We will not be as strong as we could have been with our struggles and we would never fly.

Truly, there are no shortcuts to real success in life. We do not gain the confidence through the trophies or the medals we win, but through the struggle we experience. Failing to achieve the desired results in good struggles with whole heart gives us much more confidence than the wins with short cuts and ease.

Being kind is good, but not allowing people to develop their abilities by spoon-feeding is dangerous. Let us hold ourselves back when we next time feel like doing the school work of our younger ones or buying the science model from the market instead of letting them struggle and exercise their creativity. Let the kids apply their own mind to come up with something wonderful. If we are facing some challenges in our lives, let us embrace those and fight with whole heart. The results are important but the experience can be even more critical. Let us embrace the challenges and don't be too kind.

Remember what the World Champion of Public Speaking 2001, Darren LaCroix said, ***"If you take away my struggles, you take away my growth."***

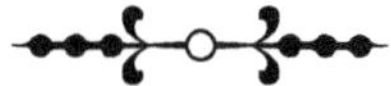

14

The Cockroach Syndrome!

At a restaurant, a cockroach suddenly flew from somewhere and sat on a lady. She started screaming out of fear. With a panic-stricken face and a trembling voice, she started jumping, with both her hands desperately trying to get rid of the cockroach. Her reaction was contagious and everyone in her group got panicky.

The lady finally managed to push the cockroach away but it landed on a man in the group.

Now, it was his turn to continue the drama. The waiter had to rush forward to their rescue.

In the relay of throwing, the cockroach next fell upon the waiter. The waiter stood firm, composed himself and observed the behavior of the cockroach on his shirt. When he was confident enough, he grabbed it with his fingers and threw it out from the door.

Was the cockroach responsible for this histrionic behavior of the people?

If so, why the waiter was not disturbed?

He handled it near to perfection, without any chaos. It is not the cockroach, but the inability of the people to handle the disturbance caused by the cockroach that disturbed the group.

It is not the shouting of our parents or boss or spouse or even the clients that disturbs us, but it's our inability to handle the disturbances caused by their shouting that disturbs us. In many multi-national companies the low times become education times for some people; they learn new skills, explore new business avenues, get trained and helps their teams be better at what they do whereas for few others this time becomes a bench-time with only task of complaining about having no job to do. The professionals who consider themselves on bench have higher sense of insecurities whereas people who are busy working on themselves and their teams are always confident. More than the problem, it's our reaction to the problem that creates chaos in our lives.

Events are state-of-affairs around us and these state-of-affairs have powers to disturb our state-of-mind. However, the question is whether state-of-affairs controls our state-of-mind or state-of-mind controls the state-of-affairs. Sure, you would say that state-of-mind should control state-of-affairs. Then, why we react on small things in life, which don't even matter an iota? Think about it.

Calmness is the cradle of power.   ***– Anonymous***

15

Potatoes, Eggs
And Coffee Beans!

Once upon a time, there was a boy who always complained to his mother that his life was miserable and he had no clue how he was going to handle it. He was tired of fighting and struggling all the time. It seemed as one problem was just solved and another one soon followed.

His mother took him to the house kitchen. She filled three identical pots with water and placed each on a high fire. Once the three pots began to boil, she placed potatoes in the first pot, eggs in the second pot and ground coffee beans in the third pot.

She then let those boil without saying a word to her son. The son, moaned and impatiently waited, wondering what was she doing.

After twenty minutes, the mother turned off the burners. She took the potatoes out of the pot and placed them in a bowl. She pulled the eggs out and placed those in another bowl. She then ladled the coffee out and placed it in a cup. Turning to him she asked. "Son, what do you see?"

"Potatoes, eggs, and coffee," he hastily replied.

"Look closer and touch the potatoes," she said. He did and noted that these were soft. She then asked him to take an egg and break it. After pulling off the shell, he observed the hard-boiled egg. Finally, she asked him to sip the coffee. Its rich aroma brought a smile to his face.

"Mom, what does this mean?" he asked.

She then explained that the potatoes, the eggs and coffee beans had each faced the same adversity – the boiling water.

However, all three reacted differently.

The potatoes went in strong, hard, and unrelenting; but in the boiling water, these became soft and weak.

The eggs were fragile, with the thin outer shell protecting its liquid interior until it was put in the boiling water. But, it made the inside of the egg strong and hard.

However, the ground coffee beans were unique. After they were exposed to the boiling water, they changed the water and created something new.

"Which one are you," she asked her son. "When adversity knocks on your door, how do you respond? Are you a potato, an egg, or a coffee bean?"

In life, things happen around us, things happen to us, but the only things that truly matter are the ones that happen within us. When faced with adversities do we breakdown or break the adversities down and move up? It's a matter of perspective. In this story, the potatoes, eggs and coffee beans have their nature and it can't be changed. However, we as human beings have full control on the way we want to be.

Let's stop complaining, take charge and be what we want to be!

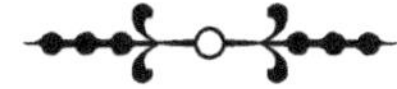

16

Be Grateful!

There was a blind boy who hated himself for being blind. He hated everyone, except his loving girlfriend. She was very caring, supportive and always there for him. He used to say that if only he could see the world, he would marry her.

One day, someone donated a pair of eyes to him and then he could see everything, including his gorgeous girlfriend. She jumped at the moment and asked him, "Now that you can see the world, will you marry me?"

The boy was shocked to see that his girlfriend was blind as well and refused to marry her.

His girlfriend walked away in tears, and later got a note sent to him saying:

"Just take care of my eyes, dear."

Human brain has a tendency to change as one's status changes. Only a few people remember what life was before and who has always been there, especially in the most painful situations.

Would we want to be like the boy who had no gratitude?

I am sure our response is a big NO.

Let us develop an attitude of gratitude and give thanks for everything that happens to us. We must know that every step forward is a step towards achieving something bigger and to be thankful. Gratitude is indeed the best attitude and a sign of noble souls. Gratitude has magic in it, let us write few gratitude notes to our people this week and experience the magic ourselves. Let us say thanks more often and we will not only make people happy but invite more reasons to be thankful from the universe. Of course, happy people around is an awesome blessing.

Gratitude unlocks the fullness of life. It turns denial into acceptance, chaos to order, confusion to clarity and enough to more. It can turn a meal into a feast, a house into a home, a stranger into a friend.

– Melody Beattie

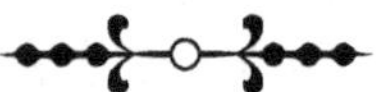

17

Stand And Walk
With Wiser Ones!

Two frogs had lived in a village all their lives. They wanted to go and explore the big city that was few miles away. They talked a lot about it for days. At last came a day when they set off to see the city. Hurray!

The journey proved to be more tiring than they expected; for, they did not know much about travelling. Halfway between the village and the city, there was a mountain which had to be climbed. The frogs decided on resting for a while and fell into a conversation.

'We must be almost there. Can you see the city?' asked one of them.

'No,' replied the other frog; 'but if I climb on your back, I might be able to see it.'

So the second frog climbed up on the back of the other frog to see the city.

As the frog put up its head, its eyes were towards upside and they turned back when the frog stood. Hence, the frog could only see what was behind and not what was on the front. Therefore, it ended up seeing the village they had just left.

'Can you see the city?', asked the frog who was below.

'Yes,' answered the other. 'I can see it. But, it looks just like our village.'

The frogs then thought that it was not worth going any further. They went back and told the other frogs around the village that they had seen the city, and it was just like their village.

The moral of the story is clear- we must stand and walk with wiser people. Whether we like it or not, people around us - influence our future. We may judge the people with their behavior, beliefs and values but not with the materials they have. Ah, we can never go wrong if we judge them with the company they keep.

The company of the good will make you good,
The company of the bad will make you bad.
Those who are of the same nature will fly off together,
Eagles soar with eagles, pigeons flutter with pigeons.

– Sheikh Jalaluddin Rumi

18

What You See, So You Get!

Once upon a time, there lived a wise old gatekeeper in a city. The old man's job was to greet the new visitors entering the city and give them required information about the routes and the trade in the city.

Travelers entering the city would stop to ask directions and availability of the work there. One day a traveler stopped at the gate and inquired of the gatekeeper, "Sir, what are the people like in your city?"

The old man paused to scratch his head before replying, "What were the people like in the town you came from?" The traveler scowled and said dryly "A terrible lot. They are self centered, greedy and dishonest."

"Well, "replied the gatekeeper with a nod of his head, "you will find them the same in our city. Don't say I didn't warn you."

About an hour later, another traveler approached the city gates. Judging by his dress and facial features, this traveler appeared to be the younger brother of the previous traveler. The old man spoke first, saying, "Judging by your looks, young man, it must have been your brother I spoke to earlier. Are you looking for him?"

The young man smiled and shook his head, answering, "No, not in this life, sir. You see, my brother has the most sour disposition. I am sad to say I don't miss his company in the least. The young man approached the old gatekeeper, offered a handshake and asked, "If you could answer my question, gatekeeper, I would be forever indebted. Judging from you age; you must know many people in this city. In your esteemed opinion, sir, what are the people like in your city?" The old man paused to scratch his head again before asking the same question, "What were the people like in the town you came from?" The traveler smiled and with joy in his voice and replied, "Oh, there can be no finer people - they are honest, hard working and generous. I hated to leave, but left to explore bigger opportunities elsewhere."

"Well", replied the gatekeeper with a smile, "you will find them the same in our city. We welcome you with open arms."

Friends, when it comes to attitude, what we choose to see is what we get. People with a bad attitude choose to look at the world through dark glasses tinted with cynicism and as a result, they mostly see only suspicious looking people lurking in the shadows. People with great attitude, on the other hand, choose to look at the world through rose-colored glasses tinted with optimism and hence, they mostly see friendly people laughing and playing in the sunshine.

No matter what happens in life, let us be good to people. Being good is the best legacy we can leave behind. Oh yes, being good becomes easy when we start seeing good in others.

The great poet Tulsi Das has summed it so well,
"जाकी रही भावना जैसी, प्रभु मूरत देखी तिन तैसी"

(People who have good inside shall see good outside and the vice versa.)

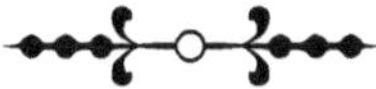

19

Delay Judgement!

Alovely little girl was holding two apples with both her hands. Her mother came in and calmly asked the little one with a smile: "My sweetie, could you give your mum one of your two apples?"

The girl looked up at her mum for a moment, she suddenly took a quick bite on one apple and then quickly on the other.

The mother felt the smile on her face freeze. She tried hard not to reveal her disappointment.

Then the little girl handed one of her bitten apples to her mother, and said: "Mummy, here you go. This is the sweeter one."

No matter who we are, how experienced we are and how knowledgeable we think we are, we should always delay our judgement about people. Give others the privilege to explain themselves. What we see and think may not be the reality.

We have read and heard about studies on how people judge others in initial few moments, just by the way they dress or talk but wait right there, because there is always something more. We must see the actions of the person and if we are not able to understand the actions too, let us go and find the intentions behind. We may have some Eureka moments when the mysteries unfold in front of our eyes. Let us always try to avoid or at least delay the judgement.

If you judge people, you have no time to love them.

– **Mother Teresa**

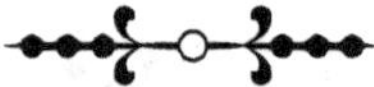

20

The Manager
Of The Largest Hotel!

George, a management trainee at a hotel, made a conscious decision to develop two great habits. One, to learn everything about hotel industry and two, to see that every customer's request is handled quickly and courteously.

On a cold, rainy night, an elderly couple entered the lobby. The gentleman approached the front desk and asked, "Young man, all the rooms in the big hotels are sold out and my wife and I need a room to rest. Could you possibly accommodate us?"

George explained to the gentleman that there were three conventions in the town and that there wasn't a single vacancy anywhere in the city. As he surveyed the disappointed looks on their faces, George reminded himself of his habit of putting the customer first, no matter what.

As the elderly couple shuffled towards the door, George called out. "We have no vacancies, but perhaps you would consider sleeping in my room this evening. I would rather have you occupy my room than have it sit vacant all night. Please, take my room. It's the least I can do for nice people on such a nasty evening."

The next morning while checking out, the gentleman said, "Young man, you are the kind of manager who should be the boss of the best hotel in the United States of America. May be someday I will build one for you." The young trainee looked at the charming couple and all three of them had a good laugh at the old man's joke.

One day George received a letter from that elderly gentleman. The letter requested that George pay a visit to him and the letter also had a round trip tickets for New York. When he reached there, the old man asked George seemingly endless questions about hotel business. Then the old man led George to the corner of Fifth Avenue, 34th Street and pointed to a marvelous new building, a huge palace of reddish stone. With twinkle in his eye, the old man turned to George and said, "This is the hotel I have built for you to manage."

George burst into laughing and congratulated the old man on his Joke. Although the old man was smiling, he wasn't laughing. "I assure you, young man", said the elderly man, "I am not Joking. I call this hotel the Waldorf - Astoria, after a long standing family name."

The old man's name was William Waldorf Astor, the heir to the one of the largest fortunes in American history. The young trainee was George C Boldt, who became the first manager of the grandest hotel of its time.

Our behavior, based on the habits we cultivate not only has the power to make people happy but also has the power to change our fortune. The seeds of good deeds we sow today, will definitely flourish into big plants in future for us. The only way to create our future is to make the present amazingly beautiful and to make sure that every person who leaves us should leave with a feeling of awesomeness. Many people waste their present on thinking about the future. Let us make our present beautiful, do good things to people and these things will come back to us in future. What goes around comes around. What we give to the world, it will give back to us.

I slept and dreamt that life was joy. I awoke and saw that life was service. I acted and behold, service was joy.

– Rabindranath Tagore

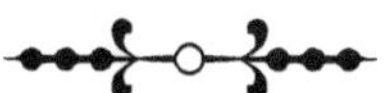

The Real Secret
Of Happiness!

A farmer in ancient China had a neighbor who was a hunter. The hunter owned a few ferocious and poorly trained hunting dogs. They jumped the fence frequently and chased the farmer's lambs. The farmer asked his neighbor to keep his dogs in check, but this fell on deaf ears.

One day when the dogs jumped the fence, they attacked and severely injured several of the lambs.

The farmer had had enough by this point. He went to the town to consult a judge who listened carefully to the story and said: "I could punish the hunter and instruct him to keep his dogs chained or lock them up. But you would lose a friend and gain an enemy. Which would you rather have, a friend or a foe for a neighbor?" The farmer replied that he preferred a friend.

"Alright, I will offer you a solution that keeps your lambs safe and will also turn your neighbor into a good friend." Having heard the judge's solution, the farmer agreed.

As soon as the farmer reached home, he immediately put the judge's suggestions to test. He took three of his cutest lambs and presented them to his neighbor's three small sons. The kids accepted with joy and began to play with them. To protect his sons' newly acquired playthings, the hunter built a strong kennel for his dogs. Since then, the dogs never bothered the farmer's lambs again.

Out of gratitude for the farmer's generosity toward his kids, the hunter often invited the farmer for feasts. The farmer reciprocated by offering lamb meat and cheese he had made. Within a short time, the neighbors developed a strong friendship.

It is certainly true that 'One can win over and influence people the best with gestures of kindness and compassion.' If we really want to accumulate more wealth and happiness, we must engrave the below beautiful words on our heart,

One catches more flies with honey than with vinegar.

– American Proverb

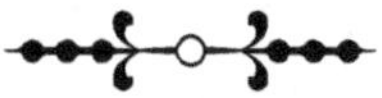

22

Inside Outside!

A father called his young son and told him that he is going to give him some work and he must do the same with excellence. He asked him to paint the railing that surrounded their house with white paint. The young boy was very excited and he acquired the skill of painting from his father. After learning how to paint, he spent a whole day painting the railing. He came back and announced completion of the job to his father. His father, while inspecting the work realized that he had painted the railing from outside and not on the inside. He asked him why the railing was not painted from inside. The son answered that as people were going to see it only from the outside, it was important to paint on the outside.

The boy asked, "Who will see it from the inside?" His father answered, "My dear son, we will see it from the inside."

A profound response, isn't it? The boy grew up as Steve Jobs and he applied the lessons he learnt from his father Paul Jobs in everything he did. Steve rejected the designs of the original logic boards inside of the Apple II as the 'lines were not straight enough'. When his team asked who notices that the lines inside are not straight and what difference do they make, he said, "It makes difference to me because I know it's not straight."

The world knows Steve Jobs went on to change six industries - computing, music, communications, publishing, animation and retail. He could do it because he had confidence in his creation and he had confidence in his creation because he knew that the products Apple made were perfect even from the places no one can see. Let the small things matter as they really do.

Some people think design means how it looks but of course, if you dig deeper - it really means how it works.

– Steve Jobs

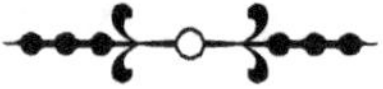

23

Hold The Touchstone!

Centuries ago, a man served a *saint* for many long years. The *saint* was really pleased with the service offered by the man for free without expecting anything in return. While lying in the death bed, the *saint* asked what the devotee would like to ask for before the *saint* dies. As the devotee had witnessed that the *saint's* blessings had real value and borne fruits for other devotees, he requested if he could get to know the secret of finding a touchstone. The touchstone was a pebble that looked like all other pebbles but could convert any metal to pure gold with just a quick touch.

Answering the devotee's question, the *saint* said that the touchstone was warm and the warmth could be felt when held in hand whereas all the other stones were cold. He also assured the servant that there was one touchstone on the banks of the river from where the man fetched drinking water to the *saint* every day.

The man really believed in the power of hard work and consistent efforts. So, he sold his few belongings, bought some basic supplies and began testing pebbles as the biggest project of his lifetime.

He knew that if he picked up ordinary cold pebbles and threw them down, he might pick up the same pebble hundreds of times again. So, when he felt one that was cold and threw it into the river. He spent a whole day doing this but none of them was the touchstone. Yet he went on and on this way. "Pick up a pebble. Cold – throw it into the river. Pick up another. Cold - Throw it into the river."

The days turned into weeks and the weeks into months. One day, however, about noon, he picked up a pebble; going with the flow and habit of throwing pebbles into the river. Before he realized what he had done, he threw it too into the river. He had formed such a strong flow of throwing each pebble into the river without thinking much that when the one he wanted came along, he still threw it away.

So it is with most of the opportunities we are presented with in our lives. Unless we are vigilant, it's easy to fail to recognize an opportunity when in hand and it's just as easy to throw it away as the pebble into the river. Even if we say yes, at times we end up not really making maximum out of the opportunities available to us. Every day is an opportunity to make our contribution in making the world a beautiful place.

In this story, the normal and cold pebbles can't be converted into warm touchstones but all the days of our lives can be converted into useful days for the world. The secret of converting every day into touchstones is, "living in the present, loving the work we do and respecting the people around."

There is a big difference between seeing an opportunity and seizing an opportunity.

– Jim Moore

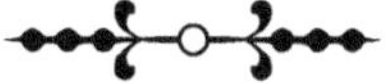

24

Power Their Aspirations!

There was a business executive who was deep in debt and could see no way out. Creditors were closing in on him. Suppliers were demanding payment. He was even finding it too difficult to pay salaries and rents. One day, he sat on a bench in a park, head in hands, wondering if there was something that could save his company from bankruptcy.

Suddenly, an old man appeared before him. "I can see that something is troubling you," he said. After listening to the executive's woes, the old man said, "I believe I can help you." He asked the man his name, wrote out a cheque, and pushed it into his hand saying, "Take this money. Meet me here exactly one year from today, and you can pay me back at that time."

Then he turned and disappeared as swiftly as he had come.

The business executive saw in his hand a cheque for $500,000, signed by John D. Rockefeller, one of the then richest men in the world.

"I can erase my money worries in an instant!" he realized. But instead, the executive decided to put the uncashed cheque in his safe. Just knowing it will give him the strength to work out a way to save his business, he thought.

With renewed optimism, he negotiated better deals and extended terms of payment. He closed several big sales. Within a few months, he was out of debt and making money once again.

Exactly one year later, he returned to the park with the uncashed cheque. At the agreed-upon time, the old man appeared. But just as the executive was about to hand back the cheque and share his success story, a nurse came running behind and grabbed the old man.

"I'm so glad I caught him!" she cried. "I hope he hasn't been bothering you. He's always been escaping from the rest home and telling people he's John D. Rockefeller."

And she led the old man away by the arm.

The astonished executive just stood there, stunned. All year long he'd been wheeling and dealing, buying and selling, convinced he had half a million dollars behind him.

Suddenly, he realized that it wasn't the money, real or imagined that had turned his life around. It was his new found self-confidence that gave him the power to achieve anything he went after.

Having some good friends at your back can make a real positive difference in our venture or the adventure. Let us always be in the company of such people who fuel our dreams, stand by our bad times and have the guts to say, 'You go ahead and live your dreams. If need be, I will be there to support'.

Even more significant question to ask ourselves is, can our friends and family bank on us? Are we the one who they feel confident of approaching when in need? What are we doing to become their power and go-to persons? It's joy to bring sunshine in someone's life? Let us lift the curtains and let the light spread.

Let us support people financially if we can, volunteer some time to help, share that hard earned wisdom from our successful or failed attempts in doing something. If none of these, at least speak a few words of encouragement to the ones who want to go for their dreams. Let us become someone's savior and our happiness is guaranteed.

Correction does much but encouragement does more.

– Goethe

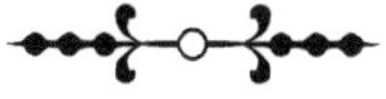

Give Your 100 Percent To Work And To People!

A boy and a girl were playing together. The boy had a collection of dolls and the girl had some chocolates. The boy told the girl that he will give her all his dolls in exchange for her chocolates. The girl agreed.

The boy kept the best of the dolls, including an automated one that could be operated with a remote control and gave the rest to the girl. The girl gave him all her chocolates as she had promised.

That night, the girl slept peacefully. But the boy couldn't sleep as he kept wondering if the girl had hidden some of the best quality and most delicious chocolates from him the way he had hidden his best operated doll.

If we don't give our hundred percent in a relationship, we'll always keep doubting if the other person has given his/her hundred percent. This is applicable for any relationship at home or at workplace. Let us give our hundred percent to everything we do and sleep peacefully.

Martin Luther King Jr. summed it so well, about giving your 100% to work, "If a man is called to be a street sweeper, he should sweep streets as Michelangelo painted or Beethoven composed music or Shakespeare wrote poetry. He should sweep streets so well that all the hosts of heaven and earth will pause to say, 'Here lived a great street sweeper who did his job well."

Relationships are about trust. If you have to play detective, it's time to move on.

– Anonymous

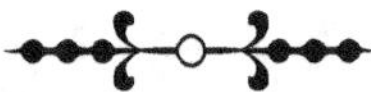

Ignore The Critics Do The Work!

One day, a father and his son took their donkey to the market in order to buy some food. The father sat on the donkey and the boy walked. As they travelled, onlookers said, "what a terrible thing, a big strong man like that riding while the poor boy has to walk."

So the father got off and he let the boy ride. Then some other people said, "How disrespectful, the old father walks while his young son enjoys the ride."

They both got on the donkey's back. And then people said, "How cruel - two people riding on the poor donkey's back."

So they both got off the donkey and walked. People said, "How foolish they are. Both of them are walking while a perfectly healthy donkey has nothing on its back."

They finally arrived at the market a day late. When they got there, everyone marveled to see the man and his son carrying the donkey.

Like the father and the son duo with the donkey, we become so concerned with the pressure we experience from people that we lose sight of where we are going and why we are going. Trivial affairs and hollow criticisms preoccupy us so completely that there is no room in our minds to see dreams, plan the course or execute one. Let us not allow this to happen to us. If we believe in our direction, it's good advice to ignore what people are saying. When we have clarity on our goals and dreams, when we know where are we going and why are we going –let us just go. People will always have to say something, at times ignoring can be the best strategy.

I don't know the key to success, but the key to failure is trying to please everybody.

– Bill Cosby

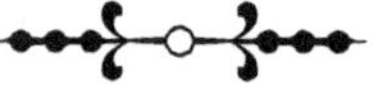

27

God Is In Details!

Shakti and Simon graduated together and joined a wholesale company where they both really worked hard.

After several years, the boss promoted Shakti to a sales manager but Simon remained a salesman. One day, Simon could not take it anymore. He tendered resignation to the boss and complained that the boss did not value the hardworking staff, but only promoted those who flattered him.

The boss knew that Simon worked very hard for all these years, but in order to help Simon realize the difference between him and Shakti, he asked Simon to do the following.

"Go and find out anyone selling watermelons in the market." Simon returned and replied that he found one. The boss asked "How much per kilogram?" Simon went back to the market to ask and returned to inform boss that it costs ₹20 per kilogram.

The boss told Simon, "I will ask Shakti the same question." Shakti went, returned and said, "Only one person sells watermelons in the town. ₹20 per kilogram, ₹180 for 10 kilograms, he has inventory of 340 watermelons. On the table there were 58 melons, every watermelon weighs about 4 kilograms, bought from South India two days ago, they are fresh, red and of a good quality. But if we wait for 3 days and reach the wholesale fruit market in the early morning on Sunday, we can buy it as inexpensive as ₹15 per kilogram."

Simon was very impressed and realized the difference between himself and Shakti. He decided not to resign but to learn from Shakti instead.

A more successful person is a better observant person, thinks more, pays attention to detail and understands in depth.

Think! Are you a detail oriented person? How detail oriented are you?

God is in details.

– Ludwig Rohe

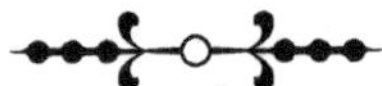

28

Keep Calm And Climb
Out Of The Crab Bucket!

A crabs supplier used to supply huge quantity of crabs all over India. During the time of low business, he decided to reduce his overheads. One day, he removed the rope that used to tie the boxes from outside. The client on the other side got very annoyed and asked, "Why did you remove the rope?" The supplier asked if the client received the crabs in promised quantity to which the client said yes.

Next time, he removed the tape as well and again, the client got annoyed, he asked for the reason of removing the tape. The supplier again responded asking if the client received the crabs in full quantity to which the client said yes.

In the similar manner, he started reducing the outer packaging and other peripherals of the packing. The client got very annoyed when he received the crabs in boxes without the lid and only covered by thin plastic sheets.

The client fumed in anger and shouted, "How dare you remove the lids? Don't you know some of the crabs may jump outside the box and I may not receive the quantity as dispatched?" The supplier again asked, "Have you received all the crabs as dispatched?" The client verified and said yes. He asked him, "Please tell me how do you know that the crabs will not come out piercing the thin plastic film if we remove all the packaging and the lid?"

The supplier answered, "My friend, crabs have a typical mentality – when one crab tries to climb up, another crab pulls its leg down."

Precisely the same thing happens in our lives. Whenever we try to do something different or work on some crazy goals, there will be people who will say, "focus on your job", "don't get caught up in taking risks", "it's not for you" or "you are not made for this", "you don't have business background" and so on. Indirectly they are pulling us down like the crabs in this story. Whenever somebody gives us an advice, please think if that person has the capability of giving an advice. Evaluate if they have ever done something similar to what we are trying and have ever faced a similar situation. If not, it will be rather helpful to take advice from the right people who have been there and done that. During journey of achieving what we want, we have to carefully choose whom to listen and whom not to. If we feel there are too many crabs around, we shouldn't even let the people around know that we are trying to escape the rut and trying to jump out of the box, instead we should just jump out.

Whoever is trying to pull us down is already below. Let us escape those, keep calm and climb out of the crab bucket.

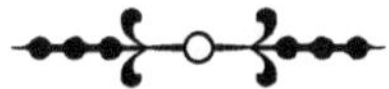

A Man's Beauty
Is In His Tongue!

Once there was a newspaper vendor who had a rude customer. Every morning, the customer would walk by, refuse to return the greetings, grab the paper off the shelf and throw the money at the vendor. The vendor would pick up the money, smile politely and say, "Thank you, sir".

One day, the vendor's assistant asked him, "Why are you always so polite with him when he is so rude to you? Why don't you throw the newspaper at him when he comes back tomorrow?" The vendor smiled and replied,

"He can't help being rude and I can't help being polite. Why should I let his rude behavior change my politeness to rudeness?"

So many people get mad on the name of tit-for-tat. Let us stop being remote-control operated machines and have control on our own behavior. The best favor you can do to yourself is to "be you", everyone else is already taken. Oh yes, we know deep down in our hearts lies kindness, love and compassion. Kindness and politeness are not overrated at all. They're underused. Let our true deeper self be dominant when we come in touch with others. Remember some people light the place as they arrive; others do so when they leave. When do you light the place? Politeness is the flower of humanity, let it blossom.

A man's beauty is in his tongue.

– Prophet Mohammed

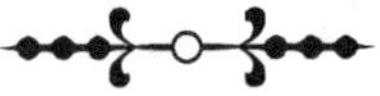

30

Kids Cry For
And Adults Die For!

Mohan was working as a security guard at a cold storage factory and used to be on his duty from 8 am to 5:30 pm. Iqbal was working as a supervisor in the factory, every morning and evening, when he passed from security gate, he used to stop by and say hello to Mohan. A lot of times, Iqbal used to spare a few minutes and engage in communication with him. He asked about Mohan's family, they also shared smiles and laughter at times. There was not a single day when Iqbal had not wished Mohan and appreciated him about his job. They developed a sweet friendship. Every morning and evening the guard would wait for Iqbal to arrive so that he could greet him.

One evening Mohan at the gate realized that it is 5:45 and Iqbal had not come out of the factory. He immediately informed his colleagues and went inside the factory. With the help of other staff, he started opening door of every refrigerator and started looking for Iqbal. After opening many refrigerators, they found Iqbal lying unconscious in one of them. He was immediately taken to the nearest hospital and his life was saved. It so happened, that Iqbal entered into a large refrigerator which was not in working condition and the door got closed by mistake. There was no way he could have opened it from the inside.

A simple gesture of wishing and appreciating the security guard saved Iqbal's life. Relationships are the foundation of our success and happiness. Every single human being has an invisible placard around his neck, "Appreciate Me". Everyone loves appreciation. These small gestures create great relationships. Relationships are not built to get benefits out of; instead they are built to give benefits to others. Every person wants to feel important and our job is to make them feel so. Appreciating people not only makes them happy but also reinforces the good they are doing. Behavior which gets appreciated gets repeated- and we help individuals become better. Appreciation is something kids cry for and adults die for. Oh yes, did we tell you - most of the times the genuine appreciation is fully free and makes a lot of difference to the recipient as well as the giver.

The roots of all goodness lie in the soil of appreciation for goodness.
– Dalai Lama

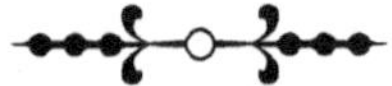

31

Be Proud Of Your Work And Master Of Your Words!

On his first day in office as President, when Abraham Lincoln began to deliver his inaugural address, one man stood up. He was a rich Aristocrat.

He said, "Mr. Lincoln, you should not forget that your father used to make shoes for my family." And the whole Senate laughed; they thought they had made a fool of Lincoln.

But certain people are made of a totally different mettle. Lincoln looked at the man directly into is eyes and said, "Sir, I know that my father used to make shoes for your family and there will be many others here who are beneficiaries of his work, because he made shoes the way nobody else can.

He was a creator. His shoes were not just shoes; he poured his soul into them.

I want to ask you, if you have any complaint, because I know how to make shoes myself.

If you have any complaint I can make you another pair of shoes. But as far as I know, nobody has ever complained about my father's shoes. He was a genius. I am proud of my father and his work."

The whole Senate was struck dumb. They could not understand what kind of man Abraham Lincoln was. He was proud because his father did his job so well that not even a single complaint had ever been heard.

Remember, "No one can hurt you without your consent." It is not what happens to us that hurts us instead it is our response that hurts us.

Let us do good in the world and be proud of every job done. Let us be a captain of our fate and a master of our words.

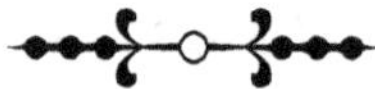

32

Empty Your Cup
So That It May Be Filled!

A brilliant young spiritual practitioner went to meet a famous Zen master to have a discussion with him on Zen. He found himself in front of a modest house. He rang the doorbell and waited. A while later, he heard shuffling footsteps and the door was opened by the Zen master.

He invited the spiritual practitioner to sit with him on the dining table. The spiritual practitioner was a little disappointed with the shabby appearance of the Zen master.

He started quizzing him immediately on comparative philosophies and the Zen master gave some brief answers.

When the spiritual practitioner began to debate with him on those answers, the Zen master stopped speaking and kept smiling at him. Finally, the spiritual practitioner got angry. He said, "I have come from a long distance just to understand the relevance of Zen. But apparently you have nothing to say. I have not learnt anything from you at all."

At this point, the Zen master asked the spiritual practitioner to have some tea. When the spiritual practitioner held the cup, the Zen master started pouring tea into it. After some time, the tea started spilling and the spiritual practitioner shouted, "Stop! The cup can contain no more."

The Zen master stopped, smiled and said, "Yes, you are right, cup can contain no more and we will have to empty it to fill new tea. Similarly to learn something new you have to empty your cup. A mind, full of itself can receive nothing more. How can I speak to you of Zen until you empty your mind to learn?"

Let us be a continuous learner, wherever we reach we will always have ample opportunities to learn and it can only happen when we keep an open mind to learn. Today is the time of learning, unlearning and relearning incessantly. We need to empty our cups of ego regularly and make space for fresh knowledge.

Empty your cup so that it may be filled; become devoid to gain totality.
– Bruce Lee

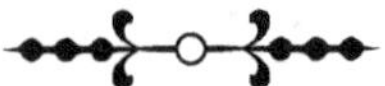

33

When Life Throws A Table Topic - Think & Act!

A wealthy man decided to go on a safari in Africa. He took his faithful pet dog along for company. One day the dog started chasing butterflies and not before long, he discovered that he was lost. Wandering around, he noticed a leopard heading rapidly in his direction with the obvious intention of gobbling him up.

The dog sensed the trouble. Then he noticed some bones on the ground close by and immediately settled down to chew on the bones with his back to the approaching leopard.

Just as the leopard was about to leap, the dog exclaimed loudly, "Wow, that was one delicious leopard. I wonder if there are any more around here."

Hearing this, the leopard halted his attack in mid stride, as a look of terror came over him, and slinked away into the trees.

"Phew", said the leopard. "That was close. That dog nearly had me."

Meanwhile, a monkey who was watching the whole scene from a nearby tree, figured that he could put his instincts to good use and trade it for protection from the leopard.

So, off he went. But the dog saw him heading after the leopard with great speed and figured that something must be up. The monkey soon caught up with the leopard, spilled the beans and struck a deal for himself with the leopard.

The leopard was furious at being made a fool of and said, "Here monkey, hop on my back and see what's going to happen to that conniving canine."

Now the dog saw the leopard coming with the monkey on his back, and thought, "What am I going to do now?" But instead of running, the dog sat down with his back to his attackers pretending he hasn't seen them yet.

Just when they got close enough to hear, the dog said, "Where's that monkey? I just can never trust him. I sent him off half an hour ago to bring me another leopard, and he's still not back".

Hearing this, leopard darted off to safety.

Whatever maybe the situation in life, if we keep our calm and composed demeanor, we can come out of it.

When Life Throws A Table Topic - Think & Act!

At Toastmasters Club meetings when one is given a topic, one needs to think and speak but in life when faced with table-topics like situations, we need to think and act.

Think like a man of action, act like a man of thought.

– Henri Bergson

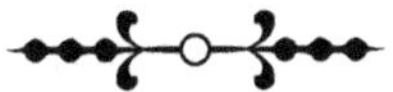

34

Get Into
The Right Rut!

There was a group of friends who regularly used to go on hunting expeditions in the Northlands of Canada every July. The place usually doesn't get much traffic. In July, dirt roads begin to soften, and as the traffic picked up, each passing vehicle would dig a deeper rut in the muddy road. By the end of the short summer, the mud ruts would be several feet deep. Once the long winter set in, the ruts would freeze as hard as cement. Frozen rut on one of the back roads got so deep that the park service posted this sign at the start of the road *"Driver, please choose carefully which rut you drive in, because you will be in it for next 20 miles."*

Our habits are like those ruts, they are easy to get into, but very hard to get out of. It is all about making right choice before getting into that rut. It always seems difficult to get into habits that are difficult to adopt. But, once we are into these for some time, these become part of our life style.

When we are installing a habit, we need to consider the long term consequences of choosing these, because once we form a habit, the habit will form us. We also have the power to uninstall wrong habits. For uninstalling the bad habits we need to follow the same process, as uninstalling is also like forming a new habit of not doing something. It is a 21 days process of installing or uninstalling a habit, however if we miss even a single day, we will have to start it again from zero. What are we waiting for? Let's try this 21 days formula with something small to begin with and we can see the magic happening in our lives.

Let us make informed choices, let us make conscious efforts, let us tame the right ruts and be a master of our lives.

Good habits are hard to develop but easy to live with; bad habits are easy to develop but hard to live with. The habits that you have and the habits that have you will determine almost everything you achieve or fail to achieve.

– Brian Tracy

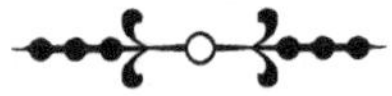

35

Exercise Your Control To Accept Or Reject The Gift!

One pleasant afternoon Buddha was walking on a road in a market. All of a sudden an angry man approached him and started speaking ill words to him. Buddha did not pay any attention and continued walking undisturbed. The man got furious and started shouting even louder. Buddha was not disturbed with his ill words and still kept walking. By now many people had gathered around. The man asked Buddha,

"I am speaking to you and why are you not getting disturbed?" He said when somebody gives you a gift and you don't accept it, whom does the gift belong to? The man responded "To him only".

"In the same way, I have not accepted your gift of ill-words. Thus, it still belongs to you." He continued, "When I have not accepted your gift why should I get bothered with it. It remains with you and you shall certainly get bothered about it later when you realize the same."

We usually get disturbed by people, who knowingly or unknowingly make unpleasant comments about us or to us. We spend huge amount of time and energy worrying about those words and deliberating with others why people are saying so about us. We can't control others. What they do or what they say is certainly beyond our control. We can only control our mind whether to get disturbed by the words of other people or to remain calm.

It is all about making our state-of-mind strong instead of worrying about state-of-affairs. Our state-of-mind should control state-of-affairs and not otherwise. Oh yes, anger does no good to us. Instead it does a lot of harm.

Holding onto anger is like drinking poison and expecting the other person to die.

– Buddha

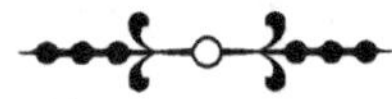

36

Make A Living
And Make A Life Too!

There was a little boy named Rehmaan who was suffering from a disease and needed blood from his elder sister Zoya, who had miraculously survived the same disease and had developed the antibodies needed to combat the illness. The doctor explained the situation to Zoya and asked the girl if she would be willing to give blood to her brother. The doctor saw her hesitate for only a moment before taking a deep breath and saying, "Yes, I'll do it if it saves my brother, Rehmaan."

As the transfusion took place, Zoya lay in the bed next to her brother and smiled.

Then her face grew pale and her smile faded. She looked up at the doctor and asked with a trembling voice, "Will I start to die right away?"

Being so young, the girl had misunderstood the doctor. She thought she was going to give her brother all of her blood and then die.

How many times we misunderstand charity. We don't really need to give all our hard-earned wealth and become poor. Even a pair of shoes to a needy person or just a ₹10 tip to the rickshaw-puller can bring happiness to our hearts and make a difference to the receiver. All the respect, wealth and wisdom we have garnered, is from the world only. Let's give it back and it's sure that the universe returns it only manifold. Donate some amount, few items of need to the needy and yes, above all if you find someone without a smile today, 'just give one of yours'!

Many people ask, "Shall we publicize the donations or do it discreetly". Well, it depends; if you publicizing your donations inspires more people in the society to contribute – go ahead and do that. However, we should not publicize only for the sake of becoming popular or feeding our ego. And yes, giving is not just about making a donation; it's about making a difference.

We make a living by what we get but we make a life by what we give.

–Winston Churchill

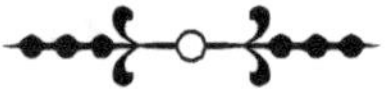

Go Together
Go Far!

There once was a farmer who grew award-winning corn. Each year he entered his corn in the national fair where it won a gold medal and became topic of the talk in the town.

One year a newspaper reporter interviewed the farmer and learned something interesting about how he grew it. The reporter discovered that the farmer shared seeds of the same corn with his neighbors.

"How can you afford to share your best corn seeds with your neighbors when they are also entering their corn in competition with yours each year?" the reporter asked.

The farmer shared, "The wind picks up pollen from the ripening corn and swirls it from farm to farm. If my neighbors grow inferior corn, cross-pollination will steadily degrade the quality of my corn. If I am to grow good corn, I must help my neighbors grow good corn."

He was aware of the power of connection in life. His corn cannot improve unless his neighbor's corn improves.

So it is with our lives. Those who want to live well must help others to live well. For, the value of a life is measured by the lives it touches. Those who desire to be happy must help others to find happiness, for the welfare of each is interdependent on the welfare of all.

The lesson here is this: If we want massive success in our lives we must help our friends and family to be successful. Don't get us wrong, inspiring others and living by example come at forefront when we talk about helping others to succeed. A caterpillar can't really inspire its fellow caterpillars to become butterflies until it becomes one. We cannot inspire others to rise to greatness until we become a role model. Tread the journey to success together. Succeeding together is fun.

If you want to go fast, go alone;

If you want to go far, go together.

– African Proverb

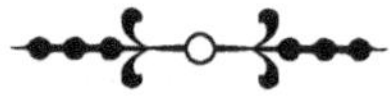

38

Don't React, Be Cool!

Acarpenter shut down his workshop after a day's job. A black wandering poisonous cobra entered his workshop.

The cobra was hungry and did hope to find its dinner lurking somewhere within. It wriggled from one end to another and accidentally bumped into a sharp-edged metal axe resulting in slight injury.

In anger and seeking revenge, the cobra bit the axe with full force. What could a bite to a sharp metal axe do? The cobra's mouth started bleeding.

Out of fury and arrogance, the cobra tried its best to strangle and kill the object that was causing it pain by wrapping itself very tightly around the blades.

The next day when the carpenter opened the workshop, he found a seriously cut, dead cobra wrapped around the axe blades.

The cobra died not because of someone else's fault but because of its own anger, wrath and ego.

Sometimes when angry, we try to cause harm to others but as time passes by, we realize that we have caused more harm to ourselves.

For a happy life, we should learn to ignore and overlook some things, some people, some incidents, some affairs and some matters.

It is not necessary that we create a reaction for every action. Let us step back and ask ourselves if the matter is really worth responding or reacting to. At times people act only to teach someone a lesson or to take revenge. Let us not bother to teach a lesson to anyone out there instead get busy in crafting massive success for ourselves.

*If we still feel like taking revenge ever in life, we can go ahead and do that as per the words from famous and successful American singer Frank Sinatra, **"The best revenge is massive success"**.*

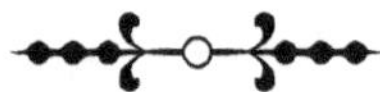

39

Consider Life As Do-It-Yourself Project!

An elderly excellent builder worked for a king. He worked with full loyalty to the king for five decades and was ready to retire now. He told the king of his plans to leave the house building job and live a more peaceful life with his family and specially enjoy his time with his grandchildren. He would miss the pay-cheque, but he needed to retire.

The king was sorry to see his good worker go and asked if he could build just one more house as a personal favor. The builder said yes, but in time it was easy to see that his heart was not in his work. He resorted to shoddy workmanship and used inferior materials, there was no finishing in the work and it was pretty clear from the structure as well as finishing that the house is not built by full head and heart. It was an unfortunate way to end his career.

Somehow, the builder finished his work and the king came to inspect the house. The king thanked the builder for agreeing to build this last house and handed the front-door key to the builder. "This is your house," he said, "my gift to you."

What a shock! What a shame! If he had only known he was building his own house, he would have done it all so differently. Now he had to live in the house he had built none too well.

So it is with us. We build our lives in a distracted way, reacting rather than acting, willing to put up less than the best. At important points we do not give the job our best effort. Then with a shock we look at the situation we have created and find that we are now living in the house we have built none too well. If we had realized, we would have done it differently.

Let us think of ourselves as builders and our lives as the houses. Each day, we hammer a nail, place a board or put some bricks and erect a wall, let us build wisely. It is the only life we will ever build. Even if we live in it for small time, that time deserves to be lived graciously and with dignity.

"Life is a do-it-yourself project." Our lives tomorrow will be the result of the things we do today. Let us wear the best attitude, make the best choices and put in our best efforts to make lives beautiful. We will live in it with pride and peace forever.

We are what we repeatedly do. Excellence, then, is not an act, but a habit.
– Aristotle

40

Face Your Fears!

Once a troop of monkeys surrounded Swami Vivekananda making him unable to move. He managed to run and to his disbelief even the monkeys ran after him. He ran faster and so did the monkeys. He couldn't find a way to escape and continued running. An old monk called out to him and said, "Don't run, face the brutes!" What happened later is a well-known part of the story. Swami Vivekananda stopped running, turned back and faced the monkeys; the monkeys fled away. Hence proving that most of the times the best way to get out of fears and problems is to face those.

What if he had not turned to face the monkeys, let's say he would run for miles and find those monkeys not behind him anymore? What would have he felt? He would have thanked God for saving his life, maybe discover a new way to get rid of monkeys for the next time or maybe even decide not to follow that route again in his life. Yet, he would have been afraid of monkeys throughout his life. One more type of fear would have added to his mind, only weakening his confidence.

But what he felt after facing the monkeys has added a lot of positive self-belief to his attitude. It also developed a sense of self-belief, the feeling of handling fear, a changed insight on how to handle problems better and much more. What he earned by facing the monkeys was much more than what he would have earned by escaping. The decision to face the monkeys set the perfect end result for him. It sure is a very small incident, but not to forget this small incident brought a major impact in his life. Swami Vivekananda fondly shared this to many of his disciples throughout his life and preached them to face their fears.

We are offered with the similar kind of incidents in life where we let the moments of fear conquer us. At first it slowly comforts us and eventually it consumes us.

It's absolutely okay to be afraid of something, it's okay to let that emotion comfort us, but we must make sure not to get carried away by the same emotions of fear. Courage isn't the absence of fear, it is the way we handle the fear. Sure, Vivekananda would have been fearful even when he faced the monkeys yet he did that. Exactly, that's courage. It's never easy to face our fears all at once. It takes time, it takes practice and not to miss, it takes more fears, but once we face these we realize lot of strength we have within.

"Face the brutes" - that is a lesson for life; Face the terrible and face that boldly. Like the monkeys, the hardships of life fall back when we cease to flee before them.

– Swami Vivekananda

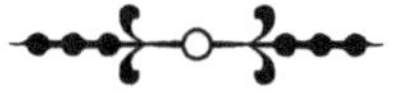

41

Be Humble!

One day a rich father took his son on a trip to the country with the firm purpose to show how poor people can be. They spent a day and a night on the farm of a very poor family.

When they got back from their trip, the father asked his son, "How was the trip?"

"Very good Dad!" replied the son.

"Did you see how poor people live?" the father asked. "Yeah!" exclaimed the son.

"And what did you learn?" asked the father.

The son answered, "I saw that we have a dog at home, and they have four. We have a pool that reaches to the middle of the garden; they have a creek that has no end. We have imported lamps in the garden; they have the stars in the sky. Our patio reaches to the front yard; they have a whole horizon."

When the little boy was finished, his father was speechless. His son added, "Thanks, Dad, for showing me how poor we are!"

Isn't it true that our happiness depends on the way we look at things? If we have love, friends, family, health, good humor and a positive attitude towards life – we've got everything! We can't buy any of these things with money. We may have all the material possessions and provision for the future as well; but if we are poor of spirit, we have nothing!

We should have compassion for fellow human beings. Respect the souls and not the financial status. Times change and today's poor kid can be tomorrow's billionaire. Let us value and teach our kids to value the things which really count in life. If we are blessed with more, share with people around.

Remember what Einstein said, "Not everything that counts can be counted, and not everything that can be counted counts." Being humble is one such thing which can't be counted but really does count when it comes to leaving a legacy.

Be humble. Period.

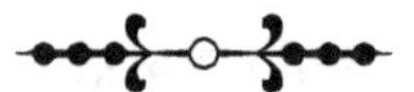

42

What Makes You Fly!

A ten year old dark complexioned boy stood outside his house depressed and looking at the balloon seller who was selling balloons of different colors.

He was depressed because his classmates used to bully him every day on his dark complexion. They used to tell him that he can't play with them; they will not even sit with him and so on.

Looking at balloons, he gathered some courage and asked the balloon seller, "Uncle, will this black balloon also fly in the air like other colored balloons?" The balloon seller was surprised on his question but quickly understood his concern.

He answered "My dear son, it is not the color of the balloon that makes it fly instead it is the air inside the balloon that makes it fly."

Whoever we are, wherever we have come from, whatever is our background, if we decide to make our dreams come true, we have the power within us to do so. We just need to identify the potential and unleash the same. Being able to move our mountains - is not a function of our background or our complexion instead it's a matter of our attitude and actions. We can change our destiny by changing our attitude and actions. To shape a life of fulfillment – let us forget everything and remember just this:

What lies behind us and what lies ahead of us are tiny matters compared to what lies within us.

– Emerson

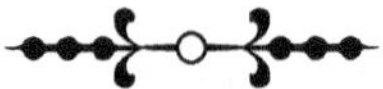

The Muddy Water!

Once Buddha was walking from one town to another with his followers. While they were traveling, they happened to pass by a lake. The troop stopped there and Buddha told one of his disciples, "I am thirsty. Please get me some water from that lake".

The disciple walked up to the lake. When he reached the lake, he noticed that a bullock cart just started crossing the lake right at the edge of it. As a result, the water became very muddy and turbid. The disciple thought, "How can I give this muddy water to Buddha for drinking?" So he came back and told Buddha, "The water in the lake there is very muddy. I don't think it is potable".

Buddha said, "Let us take a little rest here by the tree". After about half an hour, again Buddha asked the same disciple to go back to the lake and get him some water to drink. The disciple obediently went back to the lake. This time he found that the lake had absolutely clear water in it. The mud had settled down and the water above it looked fit to drink. He collected some water in a pot and brought it to Buddha.

Buddha looked at the water and said to the disciple, "See, you let the water be and the mud settled down on its own. You got clear water without any external effort".

Our mind is also like the water in the lake. When we have pressure and challenges it gets disturbed. But it is important to just let it be. Give it a little time. It will settle down on its own. You don't have to put in any effort to calm it down. We can judge better and make right decisions of our lives when we are calm and composed.

Calm mind brings inner strength and self-confidence.

– Dalai Lama

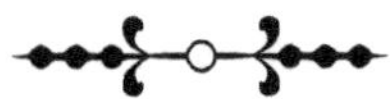

44

Too Much Care
Is Not Good!

Once upon a time, a retired teacher and an insurance agent lived as neighbors. They had their home gardens side by side and both of them had planted some plants in their respective gardens. The retired teacher was giving a small amount of water to his plants and didn't always give extra attention to them, while the insurance agent used to give lot of water and take extra care of his plants. Perhaps he was habitual of always selling more insurance plans to people than they needed.

The retired teacher's plants were simple but looked good. The insurance agent's plants were much fuller and greener. One day, during the night, there was a heavy rain and a wind due to a minor storm. Next morning, both of the neighbors came out to inspect the damage in their gardens. The insurance agent saw that his plants came off from the roots and were totally destroyed. But, the retired teacher's plants were not damaged at all and were standing firm.

The insurance agent was surprised to see it. He went to the retired teacher and asked, "We both grew the same plants together, I actually looked after my plants better than you did for yours and even gave them more water. Still, my plants came off from the roots, while yours didn't. How is that possible?"

The retired teacher smiled and said, "You gave your plants more attention and water, but because of that they didn't need to work themselves for it. You made it easy for them. While I gave them just an adequate amount of water and let their roots search for more. Because of that, their roots went deeper and that made their position stronger. That is why my plants survived".

Our children are like plants. If everything is given to them too easily and in surplus, they will not understand the hard work it takes to earn those things. They will not learn to work themselves and respect it. Sometimes it is best to guide them to get things instead of giving the things. Teach them how to walk, but let them figure out a path and learn in the process.

Loving too much, caring too much and expecting too much from someone are the key ingredients that will lead you to being hurt, disappointment and pain. *– Unknown*

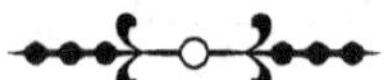

45

Who Packed Your Parachute!

One day, when Plumb and his wife were sitting in a restaurant, a man at another table came up and said, "You're Plumb! You flew jet fighters in Vietnam from the aircraft carrier Kitty Hawk. You were shot down!" "How in the world did you know that?" asked Plumb. "I packed your parachute," the man replied. Plumb gasped in surprise and gratitude. The man pumped his hand and said, "I guess it worked!" Plumb assured him, "It sure did. If your parachute hadn't worked, I wouldn't be here today."

Plumb couldn't sleep that night, thinking about that man. Plumb says, "I kept wondering what he might have looked like in a Navy uniform: a white hat, a bib in the back and bell-bottom trousers. I wonder how many times I might have seen him and not even said 'Good morning,' 'how are you?' or anything because, you see, I was a fighter pilot and he was just a sailor." Plumb thought of the many hours the sailor had spent on a long wooden table in the bowels of the ship, carefully weaving the shrouds and folding the silks of each chute, holding in his hands each time the fate of someone he didn't know.

"Who's packing your parachute?" Everyone has someone, who provides what they need to make it through the day. Plumb also pointed out that he needed many kinds of parachutes when his plane was shot down over enemy's territory. He needed his physical parachute, his mental parachute, his emotional parachute and his spiritual parachute. He called on all these supports before reaching safety.

Sometimes in the daily challenges that life gives us, we miss what is really important. We may fail to say hello, please, or thank you, congratulate someone on something wonderful that has happened to them, give a compliment, or just do something nice for no reason. As we go through this week, this month, this year, let us recognize people who pack our parachute.

Even more important question to ask ourselves is, "Whose parachutes are we packing and how well are we packing those?"

Gratitude is when memory is stored in the heart and not in the mind. **– Lionel Hampton**

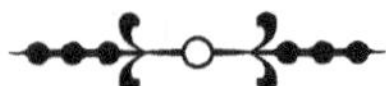

46

The Entitlement Mentality!

One academically bright young man applied for a managerial position in a big company.

He passed the first few interviews and the director did the last interview to make a decision.

The director discovered from the resume that the candidate's academic achievements were excellent all the way, from the secondary school until the postgraduate research, never had a year when he did not score very well.

The director asked, "Did you obtain any scholarships in school and college?" the youth answered "None".

The director asked, "Was it your father who paid for your education expenses?" The youth answered, "My father passed away when I was one year old, it was my mother who paid for my education.

The director asked, "Where did your mother work?" The young man answered, "My mother worked as clothes cleaner. The director requested the young candidate to show his hands. The young man showed his pair of hands that were smooth and perfect.

The director asked, "Have you ever helped your mother wash the clothes before?" The young man answered, "Never, my mother always wanted me to study and read more books. Furthermore, my mother can wash clothes faster and better than me."

The director said, "I have a request, when you go back home today, clean her hands and then see me tomorrow morning."

The candidate felt that his chance of landing the job was high and followed as he was asked to. He went back and happily requested his mother to let him clean her hands. His mother felt strange and with mixed feelings, she showed her hands to the young boy.

The son cleaned his mother's hands slowly. His tears fell over his cheeks as he did that. It was the first time he noticed that his mother's hands were so wrinkled and there were so many bruises in her hands. Some bruises were so painful that his mother shivered when they were cleaned with warm water.

This was the first time the young man realized that it was this pair of hands that washed the clothes everyday to enable him to pay the school and college fees. The bruises in the mother's hands were the price that the mother had to pay for her son's graduation, academic excellence and his future.

After finishing the cleaning of his mother's hands, the young man quietly washed all the remaining clothes for his mother. That night, mother and son talked for a very long time.

Next morning, the young man went to the see the director as promised.

The director noticed the tears in the young man's eyes and asked, "Can you tell me what did you do and learn yesterday at your house?"

The youth answered, "I cleaned my mother's hands and also finished cleaning all the remaining clothes'.

The director asked, "Please tell me your learning."

The young man said, "I learned a lot from the kind exercise suggested by you. I realized how difficult and tough it is to get something done. It takes away lot of your energy and best of the life. We should not take people for granted and every action of kindness must be appreciated. Without my mother's sacrifice there would not have been a successful me."

He further added, "just because I am her son, she gave up all pleasures of her life and sacrificed everything for my future, I am sure all fathers, mothers and other elders do the same for their family, especially kids. When the kids grow up, they must make conscious attempts to give back and live with a sense of gratitude."

"We must not have the entitlement mentality but accept things with a heart full of gratitude", and he broke into tears. These were the tears of gratitude to her mother.

The director said, "This is what I am looking for, in my new manager. I want to recruit a person who can appreciate the help of others, a person who knows the sufferings of others to get things done and a person who would not put money as his only goal in life. You are hired, my friend."

This young man worked very hard and grew up the ladder to become the most respected CEO of the organization ever. The company's performance improved tremendously and most of all the sense of gratitude and happiness among all employees became an integral part of the culture of the organization.

A child, who has been protected and habitually given whatever he wanted, may develop "entitlement mentality" and may always put him-self first. He would be ignorant of his parent's efforts and the contribution made by the society. When he starts work, he assumes that every person must listen to him; when he becomes a manager, he would never know the suffering of his employees and would always blame others. This kind of people may have been academically brilliant, may be successful for a while, but eventually would not feel sense of achievement.

Let us get rid of the entitlement mentality, if any. Let us be grateful for what we have and thank the people who have contributed to our successes.

No one who achieves success does so without the help of others. The wise and confident people acknowledge this help with gratitude.

– Alfred North Whitehead

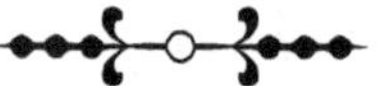

47

Are You A Prisoner, A Vacationer Or An Explorer!

A man had twin sons, Ayaan and Vihaan. Ayaan was always excited about life and very positive, whereas Vihaan was always sad and complaining. He went to a guru and requested for help. Guru told "let me first do a test on both of them." He took both the kids into two different rooms. He asked Ayaan and Vihaan to spend one hour in allotted rooms.

Vihaan's room was filled with everything that any child can dream of. It had colorful expensive toys, games, television, fancy clothes and what not. On the other hand, Ayaan's room was full with donkeys' shit.

When Vihaan's room was opened after one hour, he was crying badly and complaining about not able to find batteries for the toys, not liking the color of clothes, not able to find a channel of his choice on television and so on. When Ayaan's room was opened, to their surprise they found Ayaan full with shit from head to toe. Even his face was not visible clearly! The Guru was shocked to see him in this state and asked; "Hope everything is okay with you?" Ayaan replied, "Yeah, there was so much donkeys' shit here, I am sure donkeys find it difficult to rest at this place; so I thought of cleaning everything. All the shit has been gathered in one corner and now it can be removed from here. I hope the donkeys would love to rest in cleaner place."

Friends, there are three kinds of people in the world - prisoners, vacationers and explorers. Prisoners are the ones who are victims of their own thoughts and self created circumstances. They are always in the complaining and blaming mode. Vacationers are the ones who think that they are on this earth to pass time and whatever way they can survive it's enough. Whereas the explorers are the one who look around for possibilities and ready to explore the ways to make the world a better place. They are possibility thinkers and doers. In every situation they believe that they can discover something new and they can change things for the better. No situation or event is negative for them. In every adversity they look for opportunity.

What shoes do you fit in - prisoner, vacationer or an explorer? Oh you are reading this book and have reached so close to the end, we believe you are an explorer.

It's time to go beyond the boundaries to become a strong possibility thinker and a doer.

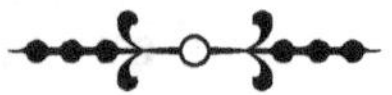

48

Don't Just Grow Old, Grow Up!

This was John's first day at B-school. During the orientation program, the students were challenged to get to know someone they didn't already know and make friends for long time.

John stood up to look around when a gentle hand touched his shoulder. He turned around to find a wrinkled, little old lady beaming up at him with a smile that lit up her entire being.

She said, "Hi handsome. My name is Rose. I'm eighty-seven years old. Can I give you a hug?"

John laughed and enthusiastically responded, "Of course you may." She gave him a giant squeeze.

"Why are you in college at such a young and innocent age, pretty woman?" John asked with a laugh.

She jokingly replied, "I'm here to meet a rich husband, get married and have a couple of kids."

"Let's see who gets lucky to be your husband from the batch," John said and both laughed out the moments. He was curious what may have motivated her to be taking on this challenge at her age.

She replied "I have a settled business and a lovely family at home but had always dreamed of having a college education and now I'm getting one".

After classes both of them usually walked to the cafeteria and shared a chocolate milkshake. They often discussed the fundamentals of few subjects, had a walk together and became friends. Every day for the next four terms of three months each, they would leave class together and talk nonstop. John always got mesmerized listening to this energy bundle as she shared her wisdom and experience with him. Oh yes, both performed very well in the academics.

Over the course of the twelve months, Rose became a campus icon and she easily made friends wherever she went. She loved to dress up and she reveled in the attention bestowed upon her from the other students, always.

At the end of the course students as well as faculty invited Rose to speak at the convocation.

As she began to deliver her prepared speech, she dropped her cue cards on the floor. Frustrated and a little embarrassed she leaned into the microphone and simply said, "I'm sorry I'm so jittery. I gave up beer for a few classmates and this whiskey is killing me! I'll never get my speech back in order so let me just tell you what I know."

As audience laughed she cleared her throat and began, "We don't stop playing because we are old; we grow old because we stop playing. There are only four secrets to staying young, being happy and achieving success.

ONE

You have to laugh and find humor every day. Life is too short to be serious.

TWO

You've got to have a dream. When you lose your dreams, you die. We have so many people walking around who are dead and don't even know it.

THREE

Anybody can grow older, that doesn't take any talent or ability but growing up is a choice. There is a huge difference between growing older and growing up. I am eighty-eight years old; if I stay in bed for a year and never do anything I will still turn eighty-nine in a year's time. But the question is 'would I grow up as well?'

FOUR

Have no regrets. In old age like mine usually people don't have regrets for what they did but regret not doing so many things they would have. And yes, the only people who fear death are those with regrets. Have no regrets, period.

She concluded her speech by courageously singing the beautiful song "The Rose."

Rose was awarded an MBA with distinction and went back to his family as an inspiration for generations to come. One week after graduation Rose died peacefully in her sleep.

Over a thousand college students, alumni and faculty attended her funeral to tribute the wonderful woman who taught so many to find humor in everyday life, have a dream, grow up with growing old and have no regrets.

Growing old is compulsory but growing up is optional.

– Bob Monkhouse

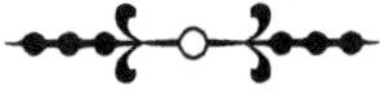

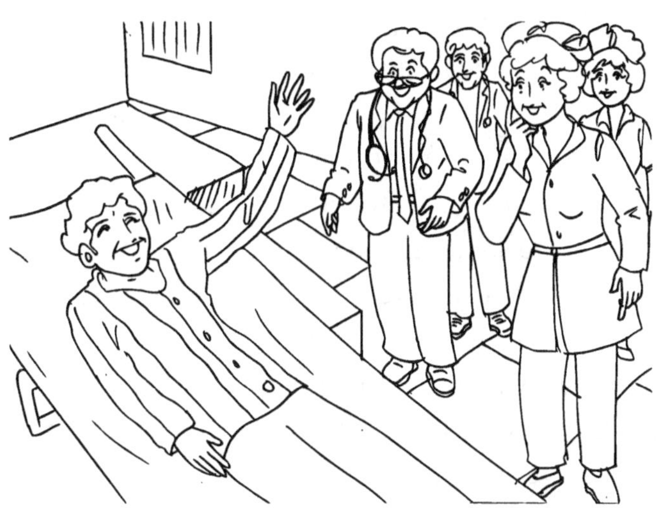

Be Miserable or Be Motivated Make Your Choice!

Thomson was the kind of manager you would follow to the hell. He was always in a good mood and always had something positive to say. When someone would ask him how he was doing, he would reply, "I am absolutely amazing; how can I be of service to you today?" He was a favorite manager to many; several waiters had followed him from job to job and restaurant to restaurant because of his positive attitude and pleasant behavior. He was a natural motivator. If an employee was having a bad day, Thomson was there telling the employee how to look on the other side of the situation which was brighter for sure. One of his curious colleagues once asked him a question, "How can you manage staying so positive always"?

Thomson replied, "Each morning I wake up and tell myself, "Thomson, you have two choices today. You can choose to be in good mood or you can choose to be in bad mood. Both cannot exist together." I choose to be in good mood. Each time something bad happens, I can choose to be a victim or I can choose to learn from it. I choose to learn from it. Every time someone comes to me complaining, I can choose to accept their complaints or I can help the fellow to find out the positive side of life. I choose to help the friends find the positive side of life."

"Life is all about choices. You choose how you react to situations. You choose how people will affect your mood. You choose to be in a good mood or bad mood. The bottom line: Quality of your life depends on the quality of choices you make."

Several years later, Thomson did something you are never supposed to do in a restaurant business: one morning he left the back door open and was held up at gunpoint by three armed robbers. While trying to open the safe, his hand, shaking from nervousness, slipped off the combination. The robbers panicked and shot him. Luckily, Thomson was found quickly by colleagues and rushed to the local trauma center.

After 18 hours of surgery and weeks of intensive care, Thomson was released from the hospital with fragments of the bullets still in his body.

One of his friends asked him, how he was, he replied, "I am absolutely awesome; tell me how can I be of service to you today?" He asked him what had gone through his mind as the robbery took place. "The first thing that went through my mind was that I should have locked the back door," Thomson replied. "Then, as I lay on the floor, I remembered that I had two choices: I could choose to live, or I could choose to die. I chose to live."

"Weren't you scared? Did you lose consciousness?" he asked.

Thomson continued, "The paramedics were great. They kept telling me I was going to be fine. But when they wheeled me into the emergency room and I saw the expressions on the faces of the doctors and nurses, I got really scared. In their eyes, I read, 'He's a dead man.' I knew I needed to take action."

"What did you do?" He asked.

"Well, there was a big, burly nurse shouting questions at me," said Thomson. "She asked if I was allergic to anything. 'Yes,' I replied. The doctors and nurses stopped working as they waited for my reply. I took a deep breath and yelled, 'Bullets!' Over their laughter, I told them, 'I am choosing to live. Operate on me as if I am alive, not dead.'"

Thomson lived. Thanks to the skill of his doctors but his amazing attitude contributed equally to his comeback. We can learn from him that every day we have the choice to live fully. *Attitude, after all, is everything. Make better choices, make better moods and live better life. If we make people feel* good they stay with us and if we make people feel bad they stay without us. We may not have control over situations but we can definitely control our responses on those.

Be miserable or motivate yourself. Whatever has to be done, it's always your choice.

– Wayne Dyer

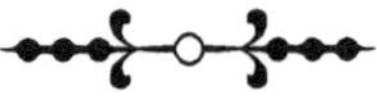

50

The Crackpots Are Good!

A water bearer had two large pots, each hung on the ends of a pole which he carried across his neck. One of the pots had a crack in it while the other pot was perfect and always delivered a full portion of water at the end of the long walk from the stream to the master's house, the cracked pot arrived only half full. For a full one year, this went on daily, with the bearer delivering only one and a half pots full of water to his master's house. Of course, the perfect pot was proud of its accomplishments, perfect to the end for which it was made. But the poor cracked pot was ashamed of its own imperfection and miserable that it was able to accomplish only half of what it had been made to do. After a whole year of what it perceived to be a bitter failure, it spoke to the water bearer one day by the stream.

"I am ashamed of myself and I want to apologize to you."

"Why?" asked the bearer. "What are you ashamed of?"

"For the past whole year I have been able to deliver only half my load because this crack in my side causes water to leak out all the way back to your master's house. Because of my flaws you don't get full value from your efforts," the pot said. The water bearer felt sorry for the old cracked pot and in his compassion he said, "As we return to the master's house, I want you to notice the beautiful flowers along the path." Indeed, as they treaded the path, the old cracked pot took notice of the beautiful wild flowers on the side of the path, and this cheered it some. But at the end of the trail, it still felt bad because it had leaked out half its load, and so again it apologized to the bearer for its failure. The bearer said to the pot, "Did you notice that there were flowers only on your side of the path, but not on the other pot's side? That's because I have always known about your flaw, and I took advantage of it. I planted flower seeds on your side of the path, and every day while we walked back from the stream, you've watered them. For so many months, I have been able to pick these beautiful flowers to decorate my master's table. Without you being just the way you are, he would not have this beauty to grace his house."

Each one of us has our own unique flaws. We're all cracked pots. But if we allow, the lord will use our flaws to grace the house. In God's great economy, nothing goes waste. Let us not be afraid of our flaws. Acknowledge them and allow

Him to take advantage of them. We too, can be the cause of beauty in His pathway. We can turn our weaknesses into strengths.

Just to give you a modern age analogy, so many people in metropolitan cities complain about traffic jams that the jams waste lot of time. Certainly the traffic jams waste time, energy and fuel. But there are people who use this time to get educated through listening to audio books and have accumulated so much wealth of knowledge. As a result they have grown in their career. They say, had it not been the traffic jams for long hours we would not have been able to finish so much of education which gives us an edge over competition.

Let us stop complaining; instead make the best use of whatever talents or situations we are presented with. Let us believe that, most of the so called cracks in our personalities or work/home environments can either be fixed or used for someone's welfare.

I have my flaws too, but I am a professional who doesn't like to miss or lose.

– Cristiano Ronaldo

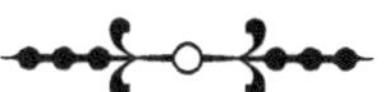

51

God Brews Coffee
Does Not Make Cups!

A group of alumni of a prestigious management institute, highly established in their careers, got together to visit their old university professor. Conversation soon turned into complaints about stress in work and life. For offering coffee to his guests, the professor went to the kitchen and returned with a large pot of coffee and an assortment of cups - porcelain, plastic, glass, crystal, some plain looking, some expensive, some exquisite and some printed with funny or motivational quotes- telling them to help themselves to the coffee.

When all the alumni had a cup of coffee in hand, the professor said, "If you noticed, all the nice looking and expensive cups were taken up, leaving behind the plain and non-fancy ones. While it is normal for you to want only the best for yourselves, that is the source of your problems and stress. Be assured that the cup itself adds no quality to the coffee. In most cases it is just more expensive and fancy looking. What all of you really wanted was coffee, not the cup, but you consciously went for the best looking cups... And then you began eyeing each other's cups."

Now consider this: Life is the coffee; the jobs, money and position in society are the cups. They are just tools to hold and contain life. The type of cup we have must not be the only criteria to define the taste of coffee. Exactly on the same analogy - the type of jobs, cars, flats and bank balance we have must not be the only criteria to define the quality of life. These sure, do impact the lives we live but we have sunrise to see, woods to walk on, good foods to eat, great books to read, wisdom to share, heart to care, friends to call and yes the family to love. Sometimes, by concentrating only on the cup, we fail to enjoy the coffee God has provided us. The happiest of the people don't have the best of everything. They just make the best of everything they have.

God brews the coffee; does not make cups. Let us enjoy our coffee.

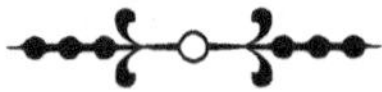

52

The Ultimate
Tool To Success!

Five frogs are sitting on a log. One decides to jump off. How many frogs are left on the log?

Four! Wrong. Deciding is not doing. There is a difference in thinking to do something, wishing to do something or even deciding to do something and actually doing. One decided to jump off but hasn't jumped and hence we still have all the five frogs on the log.

In the world of achievements and success - action was, is and will remain the king, always.

Let us remember Story# 8, about the response of a kid on glass being half empty or half full? This book offers a plethora of motivation for us to move our mountain like dreams, for us to make a mark, for us to not only realize our dreams but also to make the world a better place. Yet, theory is theory. Nothing moves until we do. Progress is the ultimate motivator and progress is function of action. Action is truly the key to success. The below poem will help us to get and stay on the action track.

If you are poor – **work**!

If you are rich – continue to **work**!

*If you are burdened with seemingly unfair responsibilities –***work**!

If you are happy – well, just continue to **work**!

Idleness gives room for doubt and fear.

If disappointment comes, please just **work**!

If your health is threatened – **work**!

When your faith and hope falters – **work**!

When your dreams are shattered and your hope seems dead - **work**!

Work*, as if your life was in peril.*

The truth is, your life really is in peril. So **work**!

No matter what ails you – **work**!

Continue to **work** *– faithfully, dedicatedly and devotedly.*

Work *with Love, Faith and Patience.*

Work *is the greatest remedy for every mental and physical affliction!*

*– **Anonymous***

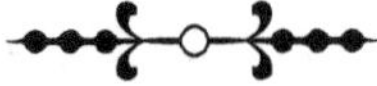

Thank you. May you live a happy and successful life.

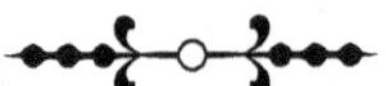

www.ingramcontent.com/pod-product-compliance
Lightning Source LLC
LaVergne TN
LVHW041320200726

843509LV00009B/556